THE CASE
OF THE
MUMMIFIED
PIGS

THE CASE OF THE MUMMIFIED PIGS

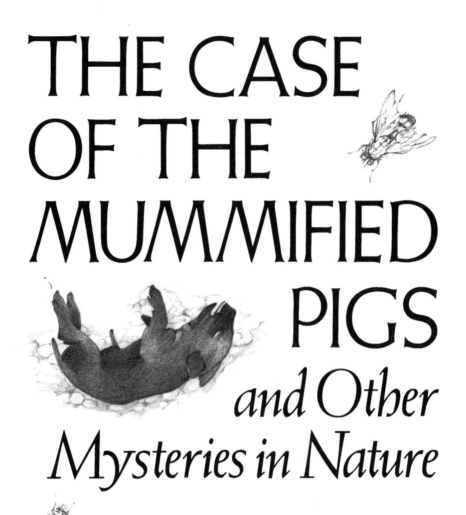

and Other Mysteries in Nature

BY SUSAN E. QUINLAN

Illustrated by Jennifer Owings Dewey

Boyds Mills Press
Honesdale, Pennsylvania

Boyds Mills Press, Inc.
815 Church Street
Honesdale, Pennsylvania 18431
Printed in China

The Library of Congress has cataloged the
hardcover edition of this book as follows:

Library of Congress Cataloging-in-Publication Data
Quinlan, Susan E.
The case of the mummified pigs : and other mysteries in nature / by
Susan E. Quinlan ; illustrated by Jennifer Owings Dewey.—1st ed.
[128]p. : ill. ; cm.
Includes index.
Summary: Description of scientific research that explains the reasons for
phenomena in nature.
ISBN: 1-878093-82-7
1. Nature—Juvenile literature. 2. Science—Juvenile literature. [1. Nature.
2. Science—Miscellanea.] I. Dewey, Jennifer Owings, ill. II. Title.
508—dc20   1995   CIP
Library of Congress Catalog Card Number 94-71027
Paperback ISBN 978-1-56397-783-1

First Boyds Mills Press paperback edition, 1999
Book designed by Abigail Johnston
The text of this book is set in 14-point Caslon.
The illustrations are done in pencil.

10 9 8 7 6

To Dr. Dale Hein,
who taught me to look for the
connections in nature
— S.E.Q.

CONTENTS

INTRODUCTION

THINK OF THE THINGS you notice when you visit a natural area, like a forest or meadow. No doubt you see trees, flowers, or other plants. Perhaps you watch an insect, or discover the tracks of a mammal, or listen to the singing of birds. You might notice clouds in the sky, feel the warmth of the sun, or wade through a puddle of water. All of the things you observe outdoors are parts of nature. But there is something else out there that you cannot easily see, though it occurs in all of Earth's forests, oceans, meadows, and deserts. It is something called the land organism.

No one can point to the land organism or take a picture of it. You will never see it on display in a zoo or museum. But it is out there, and it is quite important.

Scientists did not discover the land organism until the middle of this century. One of the first scientists to identify it was Aldo Leopold. Leopold studied deer, watched birds, hunted, fished, worked with the land, and lived in wild places for most of his life. He loved nature and wild country. Yet even he did not see the land organism at first. He discovered it only after decades of studying nature.

Leopold wrote about the land organism in the 1950s. At that time, he called it the most important scientific discovery in recent history. Few scientists agreed with him then. But today, an entire branch of science, called ecology, is dedicated to the study of the land organism. And many scientists think this research is critically important for the future of people and of life on Earth.

Scientists who study ecology are called ecologists. They are detectives who investigate mysteries in nature. Ecologists gather clues by observing plants and animals and by conducting experiments. They search carefully for connections between living and nonliving things. Based upon the information they have collected, ecologists figure out how the clues, or pieces of nature's puzzles, fit together. By solving these puzzles, ecologists have learned a little about how nature works. Their understanding of nature allows them to see the land organism.

Each chapter in this book describes a mystery that has been investigated by ecologists. As you read about each case, you will see some of the connections. Soon you will begin fitting the pieces of nature's puzzles together on your own. As you start to look at nature like an ecologist, you'll see things you didn't notice before. And perhaps, by the end of the book, you will be able to see the land organism yourself.

THE MYSTERY OF SAINT MATTHEW ISLAND

WHEN TWENTY-NINE REINDEER were released on Saint Matthew Island in 1944, the future of the herd seemed bright. This island in the midst of the Bering Sea offered plenty of plants and lichens for the reindeer to eat. No wolves, bears, or other large predators lived on the island. Biologists expected the herd to grow quickly, and it did. By 1963, just nineteen years later, the herd numbered more than six thousand animals.

Then something went terribly wrong. Sailors who visited Saint Matthew to hunt reindeer in 1965 found the island littered with reindeer skeletons. They saw only a few live reindeer.

When the sailors' disturbing report reached Dr. David Klein, a scientist who had studied the herd, he immediately made plans to investigate. Arranging transportation to the remote island was difficult. Located halfway between Alaska and Siberia, this American island is so far from anywhere that it is nearly impossible to reach. No one lives there, so the island has no airports, and it is too far offshore for small planes to venture. For most of the year, it is surrounded by polar sea ice and thus unreachable even by boat. So it was over a year before Klein and two co-workers were able to reach the island by Coast Guard ship. With camping gear, food, and a promise that they would be picked up within two weeks, the investigators were left on the lonely shore.

The first step of their investigation was to determine if the disaster report was true. On his two previous visits to Saint Matthew years before, Klein had seen small groups of reindeer everywhere. But now the island was strangely still. The bleached skeletons of reindeer lay scattered across the tundra. Klein had a few suspicions about the disaster based on his earlier trips to the island. But to solve the mystery, he needed to conduct a thorough investigation.

As a first step, the researchers explored the mountainous island. After several days of difficult hiking, they found that only forty-two live animals remained on the entire island. All of these were adult females, except one scrawny adult male. There were no calves. The absence of calves meant that the lone male was unable to sire young. So the herd was doomed to disappear completely someday. When and how had the other six thousand animals perished? And why had such a disaster happened to this once healthy herd?

Perhaps there was a clue in the reindeer skeletons. Klein noticed that nearly all of the skeletons were in the same state of decay. That meant the entire herd had died at about the same time. Based on the moss growing on the bones and their bleached condition, Klein estimated that the carcasses had lain around for at least three years. Klein had counted six thousand animals when he visited the island in summer 1963, so he concluded that the reindeer had died sometime between that summer and the summer of 1964.

Klein examined the skeletons more carefully, hoping to find more clues about the date of the die-off. He soon found the tiny, newly formed bones of baby reindeer that had died while still inside their mothers. These tiny bones told Klein that the female reindeer had died in late winter when their calves were still developing.

With the time of death narrowed down to late winter 1963-64, Klein searched for clues about the cause of death. No predators lived on the island, and people rarely visit it. So neither of these potential killers were suspects in the case.

Klein ruled out diseases and parasites because he had found almost no signs of disease or parasites on his earlier visits to Saint Matthew. And it was not possible that an infected animal from somewhere else had brought in any disease or parasite. Saint Matthew Island is too remote.

Klein found skeletons from animals of all ages. Therefore old age was not the cause of the die-off either. That left weather and starvation as possible causes.

Weather seemed likely to be involved. The 1963-64 winter had included some of the deepest snows and the coldest temperatures ever recorded in the Bering Sea area. But Klein thought a severe winter alone should not have caused such a massive die-off. Reindeer are arctic animals. As long as they have enough food, most healthy reindeer should be able to survive, even in a severe winter.

Thus Klein suspected that the Saint Matthew Island reindeer had been unhealthy or had run out of food during the winter of 1963-64. With this thought in mind, Klein looked for evidence of starvation in the skeletons. An important clue lay hidden inside the bones. A well-fed animal has fat in its bone marrow. This fatty marrow remains in the bones for five years or more after an animal dies. Knowing this, Klein cracked open the leg bones of the skeletons to examine the marrow. Bone after bone, skeleton after skeleton, the marrow was completely gone. None of the animals had fat in their bone marrow when they died. This was clear evidence that the herd had starved to death.

When Klein visited the island three years earlier, he had noticed that some important winter food plants of the reindeer looked overgrazed. When he looked around this time, he noticed more severe damage. Many of the small plants looked as if they had been clipped back. And lichens, mosslike organisms that once carpeted the island, were now absent from many areas. Klein observed that the most serious damage was on hilltops and ridges, where winds keep the ground snow-free in winter. Such places would have been used heavily by reindeer during winter.

The damaged plant life led Klein to suspect that the reindeer had run out of nutritious food. Knowing that a lack of healthy food would show up in the weights of the reindeer, Klein reviewed the records from his earlier visits to Saint Matthew. The animals he had examined in 1957

weighed 199 to 404 pounds—more than most reindeer elsewhere. Clearly, the animals had plenty of food then. In contrast, the reindeer Klein had weighed in 1963 averaged 50 to 120 pounds less in weight. These lower weights showed that when the herd had numbered six thousand animals, many of the reindeer were not getting enough to eat. Klein next weighed a few of the live reindeer that remained on the island. These animals still weighed less than normal. They were not getting enough good food. That clinched the case. Klein was now certain what had happened.

Without predators or disease to limit its numbers, the small reindeer herd had grown quickly. Many young were born, and all the animals had plenty to eat. But after a few years, there were too many animals. The reindeer ate and trampled the tundra plants and lichens faster than these could grow. Crowded onto the windswept ridges in winter, the large herd destroyed the lush lichen carpet. When the most nutritious plants and lichens became scarce, the reindeer began to lose weight. In poor condition, and with little food to sustain them, disaster was inevitable. The harsh winter of 1963-64 spelled the end for the once healthy herd. The Saint Matthew Island reindeer had literally eaten themselves out of house and home. By their numbers alone, they had destroyed their island home and their future.

When Klein and his co-workers left Saint Matthew Island, they brought with them an important understanding of the connections between animals and their environment. Populations of all living things can skyrocket in numbers, like the reindeer herd. Usually, however, animal numbers are kept in check by predators, parasites and diseases, or other factors. The mystery of the Saint Matthew Island reindeer showed that in the absence of these natural checks, a growing population eventually destroys its own environment. And disaster strikes.

THE SECRET OF THE BEAUTIFUL BUTTERFLIES

HAVE YOU EVER WATCHED a monarch butterfly flitting across a meadow? Its bright black-and-orange wing markings make this insect easy to spot. And that is rather curious, when you think about it. Most small animals spend their lives in hiding. They have color patterns that match their surroundings and help camouflage them from predators. If it is so important for other animals to hide, how do monarchs and other beautiful butterflies get away with being bright and colorful? Why aren't they quickly snatched up by birds or other predators?

Several nature detectives puzzled over this mystery. But the case was not cracked until Jane and Lincoln Brower took over the investigation. The Browers began their detective work by considering the clues gathered by previous scientists.

One clue that particularly interested the Browers was discovered more than seventy-five years earlier. In the late 1800s several naturalists observed that some insects feed on plants that are known to be poisonous to other animals. They suspected that these insects might contain the same poisons as the plants. But they had no reliable way to test these ideas.

By the time the Browers began their work, scientists had worked out ways of identifying chemicals in the laboratory. Thus the Browers were able to do something that other naturalists never could. They were able to chemically analyze poison plants and the insects that fed upon them.

The Browers chose to study the monarch butterfly because the caterpillars of this beautiful insect eat milkweed leaves. Milkweed plants contain some deadly poisons that cause heart failure and other problems in most animals. But monarch caterpillars are able to tolerate the poisons and are not harmed by eating the plants.

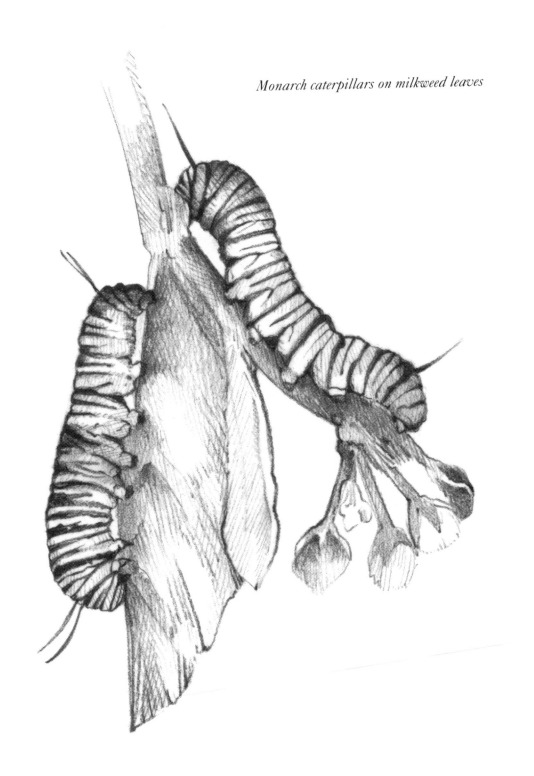

Monarch caterpillars on milkweed leaves

The Browers began their investigation by chemically analyzing a particular milkweed plant. Next they analyzed the monarch butterflies that fed on these plants as caterpillars. They found the exact same poison chemicals in the butterflies and in the plants. The Browers considered this good evidence that the butterflies were poisonous because they ate the milkweed as caterpillars. But they wanted to be absolutely positive.

So the Browers did another test. They raised some monarch caterpillars on cabbage plants. As you know, cabbage is not poisonous. When these caterpillars turned into butterflies, the Browers tested them for poisons. They were poison-free. This proved that monarchs are poisonous because, as caterpillars, they feed on a poisonous plant.

The Browers wondered what to make of this discovery. Did it do the butterflies any good to be poisonous? If an unsuspecting predator, like a bird, caught and ate a deadly poison butterfly, both would die. And that wouldn't do the monarch or the bird any good. And it wouldn't protect another monarch from being eaten by another bird. So the poison alone could not protect a monarch butterfly from predators.

However, the Browers thought, if predators knew that monarch butterflies were poison and avoided eating them, then being poison might help the butterflies survive. The scientists saw just one problem with this idea. How would a predator know which kinds of butterflies were poison and which were not?

Think about all the bottles and jars in your family's home. Some of them are full of food, but others contain poisonous cleaners. How do you know which are which? You might recognize the warning sign that is placed on containers of poisonous household cleaners. For example, you know that eating or drinking anything with a skull and crossbones sign will make you sick and might kill you. But young children often get into these clearly labeled poisons and get sick as a result. That happens because a young child does not understand the poison-warning label. Children must be taught the meaning of the poison label.

The Browers figured that predators would eat poison butterflies, too, unless they learned to recognize some warning label. Of course, poison butterflies don't have skull and crossbones labels. So what might warn predators that certain butterflies are poison?

The Browers suspected that bright colors might be a kind of warning label. In the tropics, several scientists had reported that birds and monkeys never seemed to eat the brightly colored butterflies. And one scientist had noted that many kinds of brightly colored insects fed on poisonous plants. This suggested that poisons and bright colors might go together. But could predators recognize bright colors as a poison warning?

The Browers planned an experiment to find out. They used monarch butterflies, since these are brightly colored and they had already proved that these were full of poisons. For predators, they decided to use blue jays, since these birds eat many kinds of insects, including butterflies.

The Browers first offered several captive jays some of the edible monarchs they had raised on cabbage. At first the blue jays did not touch these insects. That suggested they might already recognize the monarchs as poison. But when the Browers offered the jays little else to eat, the birds eventually began eating the butterflies. Since these monarchs had been raised on cabbage and were not poison, the blue jays did not get sick from eating them. And before long, the jays were eating the edible monarch butterflies readily, along with other foods.

Then the Browers began the second part of their experiment. They offered a poison monarch to each jay. By now the jays were used to eating monarchs, so they ate these poison ones readily. Less than twelve minutes later, however, each of the jays got sick and vomited. The Browers had suspected that the poisons might cause the birds to get sick. What they really wanted to know was whether or not the jays would remember what caused them to get sick, and avoid eating the monarchs again.

To find out, the Browers waited a while. Then they offered the jays another monarch to eat. All of the jays

refused to eat the insect—even though the ones the Browers offered this time were edible monarchs raised on cabbage. Clearly, the jays had learned that monarchs were poison.

Interestingly, now the jays also refused to eat queen and viceroy butterflies—both of which have black-and-orange markings similar to a monarch's. The Browers repeated their experiments with other kinds of birds and other kinds

of butterflies. Their experiments clearly showed that birds can and do learn that bright colors mean poison.

And that explains why butterflies with vivid colors don't have to hide from predators. A few of them get eaten from time to time by young, inexperienced predators. But most brightly colored butterflies survive by sending out a warning signal. Their colorful markings say, "Hey, predator! Don't touch me. If you eat me, you will get sick just like the last time you ate a brightly colored butterfly." Intelligent predators, like birds and monkeys, learn to read this message, so they leave the brightly colored butterflies alone.

Poison and beauty don't seem to go together naturally. Yet colorful butterflies survive because some of them eat poisonous plants and because predators learn that bright colors mean poison. Many parts of nature are tied together in curious ways.

THE MYSTERY OF THE DISAPPEARING HARES

ONE OF THE MOST PUZZLING events in the northern woods is the mysterious rise and fall in the number of snowshoe hares. About every ten years, the northern woods overflow. Bunnies line the roadways at dusk. Their tracks crisscross the snow in winter. Then, the hares die off. Areas where two thousand hares lived may suddenly contain fewer than twenty hares. For a few years hares are rarely seen. Then, about ten years later, the hordes of hares return. Weather, fire, predators, genetics, lack of food, and even sunspots have been suggested as causes of the ups and downs in hare numbers. But, over the years, scientists have found problems with each of these possible explanations.

The hare cycle remained an unsolved mystery the year that ecologist John Bryant was walking through the forests of central Alaska. The woods were overflowing with snowshoe hares when Bryant noticed something peculiar on the forest floor. New shoots of birch, aspen, and poplar had been bitten off by hares, then left uneaten on the ground. Bryant wondered why the hares had rejected their favorite foods, and he decided to investigate. He had no idea that his curiosity would lead him to the solution of one of the great unsolved mysteries of nature.

To figure out why hares weren't eating their favorite foods, Bryant snowshoed through the woods looking for clipped twigs—a sign left by feeding hares. Moose, caribou, and other animals that eat shrubs chew or nibble off the twigs, leaving a frayed branch behind. In contrast, hares have sharp front teeth and neatly clip off the twigs. Remaining branches look as though they were cut by a pair of sharp scissors.

Bryant looked carefully at all the shrub branches in several forested areas. He was surprised to find hare-clipped stems on black spruce, alder, and other plants that hares normally do not eat. But he was most surprised to find that hares were eating only the old twigs, and not the new shoots, of their favorite food plants: birch, aspen, and poplar. This made no sense. Normally hares and other browsing animals eat just the newest shoots on a plant, which happen to contain the most nutrients. Why were the hares eating only the tough old woody twigs?

Bryant looked for clues in books and articles written by other scientists. Before long he discovered a clue. Some plants make chemicals that are poisonous to plant-eating animals. Bryant wondered if the new shoots of birch, aspen, and poplar might be full of poisons.

To find out, he began looking for unusual chemicals in twigs from several kinds of plants. He found certain chemicals, called terpenes and phenolic resins, in various kinds of shrubs. The chemicals were most common in plants that hares normally don't eat, but he also found them in some branches from hare food plants. Bryant wondered if these chemicals might be poisonous to hares. So he made up an experiment to find out.

In the laboratory, Bryant took the terpenes and phenolic resins out of some new shoots of birch. He then coated these chemicals onto some willow twigs. Next he placed some coated and uncoated willow twigs at certain spots in the woods. Hungry wild hares soon visited these sites to get an easy meal. The hares quickly munched down the uncoated twigs. But they refused to touch the twigs coated with the chemicals.

In a separate experiment, Bryant offered the coated twigs to some captive hares. They refused to eat the twigs at first. But the animals that eventually nibbled on the twigs got sick and lost weight. This proved that the chemical resins were poisonous to hares.

Next Bryant studied the concentration of these chemicals in different parts of the same plants. He found that most birch, poplar, and aspen twigs contained few of the poisons. But he also found that the new shoots hares had left lying on the ground uneaten were full of the poisons. In addition, Bryant found the poisons in all the new shoots still growing on shrubs that had been heavily clipped by hares in earlier years. In contrast, new shoots on plants that hares had not clipped back remained poison-free. Based on these observations, Bryant suspected that the plants were making the poisons in response to having their branches eaten by hares.

To find out if his idea was right, Bryant designed another experiment. First he measured the concentration of chemicals in the new shoots of birch shrubs that had not been clipped by hares. As he expected, these contained few poison chemicals. Next, Bryant clipped these shrubs with a pair of large scissors, just as a hungry hare might have done with its teeth. Bryant waited for the clipped shrubs to grow new branches. Then he tested the new shoots. They were chock-full of poisons. This experiment proved that birches grow new shoots full of poisons after their branches are clipped. Bryant now knew why hares were eating the older, woody twigs. The newer shoots were full of poisons.

As Bryant thought about his discovery, he wondered if the poisons might also have something to do with the curious ups and downs in hare numbers. Many scientists suspected that lack of food caused the sudden die-offs of hares. After a boom in the hare population, the lower branches of most shrubs are neatly clipped off. So it looks as though the hares are running out of food. However, since the clipped plants quickly grow new shoots, it had always appeared that plenty of hare food was available by the end of the summer after a hare die-off. Scientists had never been able to explain why hare numbers did not increase again as soon as the hares' food plants grew back.

Now Bryant had an explanation. The new shoots of hare-clipped shrubs are so full of poisons that the hares can't eat them. Bryant eventually discovered that the new shoots of plants clipped by hares stay poisonous for two to three years. That means edible food for hares remains scarce for years, too.

Bryant concluded that hare numbers remain low until most of their food plants are once again growing lots of edible twigs. When plenty of food is available again, the hare population slowly regrows. But once hares become too

plentiful, most food plants get eaten. And the plants begin fighting back with poisons. That is when the hares once again die off. Predators, weather, disease, and other factors may also play roles in the hare cycle. But Bryant's studies showed that plant poisons are an important cause of the mysterious ups and downs in hare numbers.

Ecologists have discovered many plant chemicals that affect other living things. While certain plant chemicals affect the numbers of hares in the north, others change the way that insects grow. Still others affect the number of babies that mice have. Notably, many of the medicines and drugs used by people are chemicals made by plants. We may think plants just stand around growing leaves and flowers, but much more is going on in their green leaves. No doubt plants hold the chemical keys to many of nature's mysteries.

THE CASE
OF THE
ORANGE FEATHERS

FIELD WORKERS CAPTURE thousands of songbirds each year at the Powder Mill Bird-Banding Station in Pennsylvania. Each bird is examined and marked with a specially numbered leg band. Then it is released unharmed. Scientists band birds to learn more about them. Once in a while they learn something unexpected. That is what happened when Powder Mill workers were banding cedar waxwings.

Cedar waxwings are small songbirds named for the wax-like tips that occur on some of their wing feathers. They have jaunty crests and a mask of black feathers around their eyes. And they have beautiful tails that look as though they were dipped in buttercup yellow paint.

By 1981, Powder Mill field workers had handled thousands of cedar waxwings. So they were surprised to catch one waxwing with tail feathers tipped with bright orange instead of yellow. The next year, when several waxwings with orange tail bands turned up, the field workers contacted Dr. Kenneth Parkes. Perhaps the curator of birds at the Carnegie Museum of Natural History in Pittsburgh, Pennsylvania, could explain why these birds had orange-tipped tails.

Parkes was curious about the strange orange-tipped tail color, too. He did not know what caused it, but he wanted to learn more. He wrote to a newsletter read by bird watchers and scientists. He asked readers to write him if they saw any waxwings with orange tail feathers.

Parkes was surprised when letters from bird watchers and scientists poured in from all over the northeastern United States. The strange orange-tailed waxwings had been seen in many places. Birds do not suddenly grow different-colored feathers. What was causing the mysterious new feather color?

Parkes called Dr. Alan Brush, an expert on bird feathers, to help investigate this mystery. Brush had studied cedar waxwing feathers several years earlier. But he had never seen a waxwing with orange tail feathers. And this was the first time he had heard of such a change in the color of a wild bird. With the help of another scientist, Jocelyn Hudon, Brush began looking into the mystery.

Brush and Hudon already knew a lot about feather colors. Red, yellow, and orange feather colors are formed only by certain chemicals, called carotenoid pigments. These are the same chemicals that make carrots look orange. They are formed only by plants, not by animals. So birds can only have red, yellow, or orange feathers if they eat plants that have carotenoid pigments or if they eat animals that eat plants with the pigments.

Birds with these pigments in their feathers sometimes change color when held captive. For example, captive flamingos turn white if they are fed the wrong foods. They grow pink feathers again if they are fed a diet that includes ground-up shrimp. The shells of shrimp contain red pigments that these animals acquired from eating bits of plants.

With this knowledge in mind, Brush and Hudon made a guess. Perhaps orange-tailed birds were eating different foods than birds with normal tail colors. If so, they might get different pigments from their foods. That could cause a change in tail color.

To confirm their suspicions, the scientists studied the pigments in waxwing tail feathers. The main pigment in normal waxwing feathers was a yellow one. Orange-tailed waxwings had the yellow pigment, too. But they also contained an unusual red pigment, called rhodoxanthin.

The scientists recognized this as an important clue to the mystery. Few kinds of plants make this unusual red pigment. Brush and Hudon suspected it might be easy to figure out the source of the red pigment in waxwing tails just by testing waxwing foods. But chemical tests cost money and take a lot of time, and waxwings eat many different kinds of berries and insects. Testing all the different foods of waxwings would be impossible.

Brush and Hudon needed to do some more detective work. They carefully studied the reports of orange-tailed waxwings that Parkes had collected. Perhaps this information contained more clues. The first sightings of orange-tailed waxwings had occurred less than thirty years earlier. But the sightings had become more and more common over the years. Sightings of birds with orange-tipped tails had spread from a fairly small part of the Northeast to all parts of the region. And all the orange-tailed birds were fledglings that had recently left their parents' nests.

Brush and Hudon realized that the red pigment must come from a plant that had appeared in the Northeast at about the same time as the first sightings of orange-tailed waxwings. That was about thirty years earlier. And since all the orange-tailed waxwings were young, the pigment had to be in a plant that cedar waxwings fed their young. Cedar waxwings like to eat small red berries. And in midsummer they feed these to their young, along with insects. Brush and Hudon guessed that the unusual red pigment most likely came from a berry. But which one?

Brush contacted the Connecticut Department of Environmental Protection for help. Shortly, scientists there provided some more clues. People had brought many new kinds of plants into the Northeast from all over the world. Some of these had spread widely throughout the region. Most importantly, seven new kinds of shrubs produced red berries in midsummer when waxwings were feeding young.

Brush sensed that he was nearing an answer to the mystery. He examined berries from each of these seven plants to find out what pigments each contained. He found that all of the plants contained carotenoid pigments of some type. But only one species, the Morrow's honeysuckle, held the unusual red pigment rhodoxanthin. This plant had been brought to the Northeast from Japan about thirty years earlier. It had been planted in yards, parks, and along roadsides throughout the region.

When biologists confirmed that waxwings fed the honeysuckle berries to their young, the mystery was solved. Baby waxwings get the unusual red pigment when their

parents feed them Morrow's honeysuckle berries. This pigment settles in their growing tail feathers. The red mixes with the normal yellow pigments to create the unusual orange-tipped tail feathers. Adult waxwings grow new tail feathers in fall. Then the Morrow's honeysuckle berries are gone, so the adults eat other foods. And their new tail feathers grow out with the normal yellow tips.

By bringing Morrow's honeysuckle from Japan, people provided a new source of food for waxwings. And accidentally, they changed the tail color of young waxwings. Certainly no one expected this surprising result. Many other connections between plants and animals remain the secrets of nature. As people change the numbers and kinds of plants that cover the lands of Earth, we can only wonder what other surprising connections will someday be revealed.

THE PUZZLE IN THE POSTCARD SCENE

THE MOUNTAIN SLOPES of northern Arizona are covered with meadows of red, yellow, and violet flowers mixed with forests of white-trunked aspen trees. It is not surprising that photos of this beautiful scene appear on dozens of picture postcards and in several books on nature. Like most people, photographers see beauty when they look at the colorful mountain slopes. But two ecologists from the University of Northern Arizona looked at these same mountains and saw a mystery.

Lisa Cantor and Thomas Whitham looked at the post-card scene and wondered why the hills had meadows. Why weren't the hills completely covered by aspen trees? Normally, meadows slowly turn into forests as trees move in and shade out the grasses and flowers. Since the richest soil on the hillsides was in the meadows, it seemed odd to Cantor and Whitham that aspen trees were not growing in the meadow areas, too. The nature detectives hiked up a mountainside to investigate.

It wasn't long before the ecologists discovered a clue. They found many small dead aspen along the edge of a meadow next to a healthy grove of trees. It looked as if something in the meadow had killed these young aspen saplings. At first the ecologists had no idea what had killed the trees. Grasses and flowers carpeted most of the ground, and several mounds of fresh soil showed where pocket gophers had turned up the rich meadow dirt. The site looked just like any other part of a mountain meadow—except for the dead saplings.

Cantor and Whitham thought about the dead saplings as they walked along the edge of the aspen grove. Soon they came to an area where most of the young trees were alive rather than dead. That caught their attention.

What was different about this area? Why were most of the aspen here alive, while elsewhere most were dead? Cantor and Whitham scanned the area in search of clues.

*Dead saplings were found
near the edge of a healthy aspen grove.*

The same grasses and flowers carpeted the meadow. But there were fewer mounds of turned-up soil. Cantor and Whitham became suspicious. Fewer mounds probably meant fewer pocket gophers.

Pocket gophers spend most of their lives underground, tunneling through soft soil. They eat the roots and stems of plants. Was it possible that gophers had eaten or clipped the roots of the young aspen trees and killed them?

Cantor and Whitham knew one way to find out. The small trees on the edge of an aspen grove should be connected to the other trees in the forest. That is because an aspen forest is often a single gigantic tree with many different trunks.

A single tree that grows from a seed begins the forest. As this seed tree grows, it sends out roots in all directions. Most of the roots just gather water and nutrients. But some of the roots send up shoots that grow up to form new aspen trees. The older trees help nourish the young trees. After a while the new trees send out more roots, which send up new shoots that form more trees. Eventually an aspen forest is formed. Cantor and Whitham decided to dig up some of the dead trees and find out if they were still connected to the other aspens.

The roots on the dead saplings told the story. Several of them had no roots at all—the stems were chewed at the base. Other dead trees had normal roots. But the one main

Many aspen trees are connected by their underground roots.

root that should have connected those saplings to the forest was clipped off. So pocket gophers had killed some of the young trees on the edge of this aspen grove. Was it possible that gophers affected aspen trees elsewhere?

Cantor and Whitham decided to look at pocket gophers and aspen trees in other areas. They visited eight aspen groves. At each site, they counted the number of pocket gopher mounds and the number of dead saplings along the forest edge. Dead saplings were much more common in areas with many gopher mounds. Still, that didn't prove that the gophers had killed the trees. Perhaps there were other reasons that gophers just liked to burrow in areas where aspen trees died.

Cantor and Whitham planned an experiment. First they set up six plots along the edges between an aspen grove and a meadow. The scientists counted and measured all the sapling trees in each plot. They needed to be sure that at the start of the experiment all six plots had about the same number of saplings.

Next Cantor and Whitham built fences around three of the plots. They buried the fencing deep in the soil so that pocket gophers could not burrow under the fences. Then they trapped and removed all the pocket gophers that were inside the three fenced plots. The scientists left the gophers alone in the other three plots.

Cantor and Whitham expected aspen trees might survive a little better and grow a bit more quickly in the fenced plots without pocket gophers. But just four months later, when they visited the plots again, they were amazed to find that large differences already existed.

In the plots without gophers some trees had died. But over twice as many saplings were dead in the plots where gophers still lived. This proved that gophers were killing many young aspen. The scientists also found that the gopher-free plots had over three and a half times more new

aspen shoots than any of the plots where gophers still lived. That clearly showed that the tunneling and chewing of gophers prevented aspen trees from sending up new shoots.

The following summer Cantor and Whitham discovered that gophers had also affected the growth of surviving aspen trees. They measured the height of all the saplings in each plot and compared these heights to those they had measured at the beginning of their experiment. The saplings in the plots without gophers had grown four to five times faster than the saplings in plots where gophers were busy chewing through roots and tunneling through the soil. That sealed the case against the gophers.

Postcard scenes of northern Arizona show open stands of aspen trees mixed with flower-filled meadows. These beautiful scenes exist because of pocket gophers. Without the underground work of these little rodents, aspen trees would soon take over the hillsides and shade out the meadow flowers. What creatures do you suppose are working behind the scenes to help create the beauty in other postcard scenes of nature?

THE RIDDLE OF THE GREEN TREE ISLANDS

KARI LAINE AND PEKKA NIEMELÄ looked over the forested hillsides of northern Finland in 1979. Thousands and thousands of dead birch trees surrounded a few islands of green, living trees. Almost fifteen years earlier, in 1965, a population explosion of moths had occurred. The event was not really unusual, for outbreaks of moths occur regularly in the north. But its effects were severe. The hungry caterpillar larvae of the moths had eaten all the leaves of most of the trees in the area. The scientists were not surprised that so many trees had died, but they wondered why certain islands of trees survived. Laine and Niemelä decided to investigate this mystery.

The scientists searched for clues by looking more closely at the islands of green on the barren hillsides. Almost immediately they noticed a pattern. Every patch of living trees included a large wood-ant nest. Was it possible that ants helped the birch trees survive the caterpillar hordes?

That didn't seem very likely. Wood ants do eat caterpillars and other leaf-eating insects if they come across them. But they get most of their food by helping aphids, one of the worst insect enemies of birch trees. Aphids have special sucking mouth parts to pierce the leaves of plants and suck out their sap. In some kinds of aphids, most of the sap passes right through and dribbles out as a sweet waste material, called honeydew.

Aphid honeydew is the main food of wood ants. To make sure they have a good supply of it, the ants have a partnership with aphids. In trade for the honeydew, the ants protect aphids by attacking or eating larger insects that might eat the aphids. The ants also carry the aphids around, moving them from one place to another on a tree. These actions help the aphids grow faster and produce more young. That means more honeydew for the ants.

But it harms the birch trees. The trees need the sap stolen by the aphids and their partners in crime, the wood

Small islands of green birch trees were surrounded by many dead trees.

ants. Birch trees covered by ant-tended aphids are less healthy and grow more slowly than trees without aphids. Considering this, Laine and Niemelä wondered why the less healthy trees around ant nests had lived through the caterpillar outbreak, while most other trees had died.

To figure out what had happened, the scientists made maps showing all the old wood-ant nests and all the living, damaged, and dead birch on one hillside. The maps showed that certain trees near the ant nests had died, while some trees farther away had survived. But the maps also clearly showed that nearly all of the living trees grew within sixty-six feet of an ant nest.

The maps convinced Laine and Niemelä that ants had somehow protected most of the trees close to their nests. That was the only way to explain the overall pattern. But how did the ants protect the trees? After thinking about the problem for a while, the scientists figured that ants might help trees survive caterpillar outbreaks if they ate or drove off the caterpillars. How could the scientists find out if that happened?

They decided to look for evidence in the living trees on the hillside. If ants drove away plant-eating insects, like caterpillars, then trees growing close to ant nests should have few insect-damaged leaves. But living trees growing farther away from ant nests should have more insect damage.

The scientists collected branches from living trees at

Wood ant and aphids on birch leaves

different distances from an ant nest. They counted how many leaves on each branch had holes or chewed edges — signs of insect damage. As they suspected, trees close to ant nests generally had fewer chewed leaves than trees growing farther away.

This was good evidence that ants might be protecting the trees from leaf-eating insects. But there was one confusing piece of evidence. Certain trees close to ant nests had many damaged leaves. And some trees growing farther away had few damaged leaves. This bit of information did not quite fit the scientists' theory that ants protected the trees near their nests.

The ecologists decided to look more closely at the ants. After counting the number of ants visiting different trees and reading reports from other scientists, they discovered the answer. Wood ants visit trees covered by aphids much more often than they visit trees without aphids. The ants eat any leaf-eating insects they come across, including caterpillars. But they find more of the leaf-eaters in trees they visit often.

Laine and Niemelä concluded that the only trees that survived the hordes of caterpillars in 1965 were those near an ant nest *and* covered with aphids. Trees far away from ant nests and aphid-free trees close to ant nests had been killed by the hungry leaf-eating caterpillars.

When the scientists began their detective work, they thought that ants and their aphid partners were enemies of birch trees. But when they looked more closely, the picture was less clear. In a curious way, the ants and their aphid partners seemed to help the trees. Trees with aphids grow slowly. But in years when moth caterpillars are everywhere, the birch trees of northern Finland apparently cannot survive without aphids to attract the ants that eat or drive off the leaf-eating caterpillars. So, in the long term, aphids and wood ants help the birch trees survive. Careful detective work is always needed to uncover exactly what is going on in nature.

THE CASE OF THE MUMMIFIED PIGS

YOU HAVE PROBABLY HEARD of Egyptian mummies. They are the dried bodies of Egyptian people that have remained preserved for thousands of years. Have you ever wondered why the bodies did not decay? Nature sleuth Jerry Payne learned part of the reason when he investigated the decay of dead animals in the woods of South Carolina.

Payne had noticed that the complete bodies of dead animals were rarely found. Yet animals die every day. Squirrels die of diseases. Old deer with worn-out teeth slowly

59

starve to death. Skunks are hit by cars. And baby birds freeze to death during late spring snows. Yet we rarely find a dead animal body. Payne wondered about this and decided to investigate.

He started out by collecting the bodies of various animals killed by cars on the highway, including frogs, mice, rats, shrews, and chipmunks. He placed these bodies out in an oak and pine forest. Then he walked in the woods each day to see what had happened to the dead animals.

In some ways the woods are natural recycling centers. All living things are made up of elements bonded together in complex groups, called molecules. Certain organisms, called decomposers, break down or decay the molecules and return the elements to the soil and air where they can be used again by living things. Payne wanted to find out exactly what organisms were involved in the recycling of elements in dead animals. So he carefully observed the decay of the bodies and noted the kinds and numbers of organisms visiting the carcasses.

Payne soon found signs of bacteria at work on all the dead bodies. Bacteria are so tiny that you need a microscope to see them. But Payne did not need a microscope to tell when bacteria were active. As bacteria work, they release gases that smell awful. Payne could tell when bacteria were at work from a long way off.

Payne also found evidence of fungi at work decaying the bodies. If you've ever seen a piece of moldy bread, you have seen fungi at work. Payne found moldlike growth on many of the carcasses.

Bacteria and fungi are important decomposers, and Payne was not surprised to find them at work decaying the animals in the woods. But he was amazed by the number and variety of small animals, called invertebrates, that he found around the dead animals. Invertebrate animals include insects, spiders, centipedes, and worms. Other scientists did not think these animals were very important parts of the decay process. But based on his observations, Payne suspected that these creatures might be very important.

He guessed that dead animals might decay more slowly if invertebrate animals were kept away. To find out if his guess was correct, Payne planned an experiment. He decided to compare the decay of animal bodies open to invertebrates with the decay of animal bodies that invertebrates could not reach.

Payne needed several dead animals of the same size to make a good comparison of decay in these two situations. Local farmers probably thought Payne was crazy when he asked them for dead baby pigs, but they gave him several piglets that were born dead and some that were accidentally crushed by the mother pig soon after birth.

Payne then constructed two kinds of cages big enough to hold the dead pigs. He made a few of the cages out of wire mesh. Invertebrates, such as insects, could easily move in and out of the holes in these cages. Payne made the other cages of screen. The holes in the screen were too small for insects and other invertebrates to move through. Payne placed the dead pigs inside the two kinds of cages, then set the cages out in the woods.

He didn't have to wait long for the results of his experiments. Flies began buzzing around the cages within five minutes after he put them out. But different things happened inside the two kinds of cages.

Inside the wire cages, the dead piglets filled up with

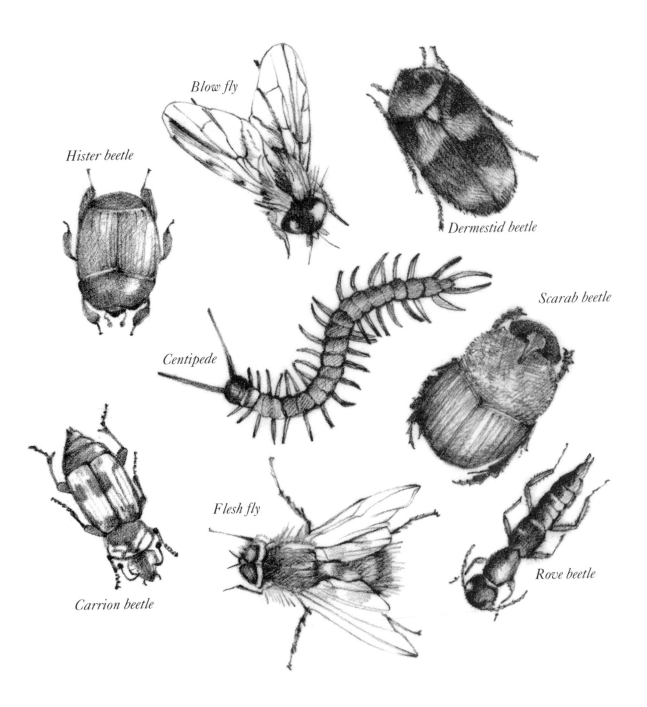

Hister beetle

Blow fly

Dermestid beetle

Centipede

Scarab beetle

Carrion beetle

Flesh fly

Rove beetle

bacterial gases within a single day. Within six days the pig bodies had mostly decayed. After eight days all that was left was a bit of dry skin, cartilage, and bones. In these few days Payne recorded 522 kinds of invertebrates visiting the bodies. Among these were 217 species of beetles and 108 kinds of flies! Wasps, ants, true bugs, moths, springtails, centipedes, millipedes, and snails were among the many invertebrate visitors. Did these animals help decay dead animals?

Events inside the screen cages provided a clear answer. There, something quite different and very strange happened. Many insects buzzed and crawled around outside the cages, but they could not get in. Microscopic bacteria and fungi could get through the screen easily. But Payne noticed that evidence of bacteria at work still did not appear for over a day and a half—twelve hours later than bacteria had shown up in the wire cages.

Eventually, though, the carcasses in the screen cages bloated with bacterial gases. But even after five days the piglet bodies in the screen cages remained in good condition. And the smell of bacteria at work faded. As more days passed, the screened-in piglet bodies slowly began to shrivel up and dry out. Instead of decaying, the screened-in piglets slowly turned into dried-out mummies. Even three months later, on the last day of Payne's study, the piglet mummies still remained intact inside the screened cages.

The screened-in piglets slowly became mummified.

Payne wasn't investigating Egyptian mummies, but his experiment explained part of the reason that Egyptian mummies exist. Ancient Egyptians carefully spread oils and spices over the bodies of certain people, then tightly wrapped the bodies in cloth. The oils, spices, and cloth worked the same way as Payne's screen cages—these kept the insects and other invertebrates away from the bodies.

As Payne's experiment clearly showed, bacteria and fungi cannot completely decay a dead body without help from invertebrates, particularly certain insects. Payne figured out three ways that insects assist in decay.

First, certain insects, such as flies, speed up decay by carrying bacteria and fungi to the body of a dead animal. Some important decomposing bacteria and fungi may never reach a dead animal without a free ride from an insect. Bacterial decay inside the screened cages began late because bacteria-carrying insects could not land on the dead piglets.

Other insects speed decay by eating dead flesh. Many kinds of flies laid their eggs on the bodies in the wire cages. The larvae that hatched from these eggs ate much of the animals' flesh. But flies could not lay their eggs on the dead bodies in the screen cages, so no flesh-eating larvae hatched out to help decay them.

In addition to bringing in bacteria and fungi and eating the flesh, many invertebrates chew holes in the skin of a dead animal. These holes allow fungi and bacteria to get through the skin and begin their work inside.

Payne's mummified pigs show the importance of insects and other invertebrates in the process of decay. Decay is nature's method of recycling elements. If dead plants and animals did not decay, the elements in them would never return to the soil and air. Eventually plants would run out of some important elements, and they could not grow. That would be a disaster for nearly all living things.

Some people don't like flies, beetles, and other invertebrates. But can you imagine what would happen if there were no invertebrates at work in nature? Nature's recycling centers just don't work without them.

THE TREES THAT WOULD NOT GROW

IN THE EARLY 1900s, S. L. Kessell headed a group of foresters who wanted to grow pine forests in western Australia. At the time no pine trees grew in that area. But Kessell and others hoped to grow forests and eventually start a logging industry in the region.

Kessell and his co-workers began their project by trying to grow pine trees from seed. They planted hundreds of pine tree seeds on the grounds of local nurseries. The seeds soon sprouted. But the seedlings grew only a few inches tall. Then they stopped growing, turned yellow, and died.

This puzzled the foresters. Vegetables and flowers planted in the same nurseries grew well. And pine trees grew well in other parts of Australia. None of the dying seedlings had any diseases or parasites. None of them showed signs of insect attack. So why wouldn't the seedlings grow?

Kessell's team first suspected that growing conditions were wrong. They tried changing the environment in the nurseries. They planted seeds in different seasons. They gave some seedlings more water. They tried shading some seedlings during the hottest weather. But none of these changes helped. The seedlings still died.

The foresters next suspected problems with the soil. They tested the soil to find out if it was right for pines. Fertilizers and minerals did not seem to be missing. The soil seemed fine for tree growth. But Kessell and the others didn't want to give up their idea of growing pine trees in western Australia. Even though their tests suggested it wouldn't help, they tried adding various fertilizers and minerals to the soil. But no kind or amount helped. The tree seedlings still died.

The mystery of the trees that wouldn't grow seemed insolvable. The foresters nearly abandoned the entire forestry project. Then someone noticed that some of the tree seedlings were not as sick as the others. These less sickly trees grew in a few scattered patches of soil.

A few of the seedlings were not as sickly as others.

Kessell's group quickly compared the soil in these patches to the soil around the more sickly trees. Their chemical tests showed no differences. Could some other kind of difference exist in the patches of soil?

Soil is made up of dirt, rocks, dead plants, and living things. A handful of soil usually contains thousands of tiny animals and millions of microscopic creatures. The foresters made a wild guess. Perhaps the seedling trees needed some living part of the soil. If so, whatever living thing was needed, it had to exist in soil around healthy pine trees. Kessell's group quickly planned an experiment to test this new idea.

They chose a small plot in one of the failing nurseries and weeded out everything except the sickly seedlings.

Next they got a bag of soil collected from beneath some healthy pine trees in another part of Australia. The foresters sprinkled this bag of soil over one-half of their plot. They did nothing to the other half. Then they waited.

In the half of the plot where soil was added, the sickly seedlings soon greened up. The seedlings in the other half of the plot withered and died. Kessell's team gathered more soil from beneath healthy trees. They scattered it in all the failing nurseries. Soon all the tree seedlings were saved, and the foresters were able to continue with their plans to grow pine forests in western Australia. However, the mystery of the trees that wouldn't grow was far from solved.

When the Australian foresters reported their findings to other scientists, they could only say that the pine trees clearly needed something from soil around healthy trees. But they had no clues to the identity of the mysterious soil factor. Fingers were pointed at many suspects. "Perhaps it was a rare mineral," said some. "Maybe it was bacteria," suggested others. Some scientists thought that the mysterious soil factor might be a mushroom.

A mushroom is just the aboveground part of certain fungi. The part of the fungi that grows and feeds usually occurs underground. It looks like fine white hairs. These hairs are called hyphae (HIGH-fee). Those who suspected that a mushroom was the mysterious soil factor pointed to

Mushroom with hyphae

fine white hairs of fungi growing around the roots of all the healthy seedlings. These hyphae did not grow on the roots of the sick seedlings.

But other scientists scoffed at the evidence. Some fungi steal food from plants. The hyphae of these parasitic fungi grow through living plants. Since the fungal hyphae found with the pines were growing around and through the seedling roots, most scientists felt certain these root fungi were harmful parasites.

Arguments over the mysterious soil factor continued. No one could say for sure why the seedlings died. And no one knew for sure why the added soil saved the sickly seedlings. The mystery was gradually forgotten. Then forty years later, in another part of the world, the mysterious soil factor struck again.

United States foresters hoped to start a logging industry for pine trees in Puerto Rico. Pine trees did not grow on this island naturally, so the foresters had to bring in seeds and grow pine trees first. They encountered the same problems the Australians had. No matter how the seedlings were treated, they turned yellow and died. After twenty years of failed attempts at raising pine seedlings, these foresters finally tried the solution the Australians had discovered. They scattered soil collected from beneath healthy pine trees in the United States around the seedlings in Puerto Rico. The mysterious soil factor saved the seedlings. And that rekindled interest in the old mystery.

James Vozzo and Edward Hacskylo of the United States Forest Service decided to find out once and for all whether mushrooms could be the mysterious soil factor. To do so, these scientists planned to add root fungi mushrooms alone to dying seedlings instead of just scattering soil that contained all kinds of things.

To prepare for their experiment, the scientists collected four kinds of mushrooms growing around pine trees in the United States. Then these scientists took these mushrooms to Puerto Rico. Once there, they baked a big batch of soil at a very high temperature to make sure that it did not contain any living things other than those they added.

The scientists planted pine seeds in several small bags of this sterilized soil. When the seeds sprouted, the scientists added spores of mushrooms to half of the bags. They did not add anything to the remaining bags of seedlings. As soon as root fungi hyphae surrounded the seedlings' roots, the scientists planted all the seedlings out in the field.

Within ten weeks the difference was obvious. The seedlings planted with the mushrooms were tall and green, and their roots were covered with hyphae. The seedlings planted without the mushrooms were small and sickly, and their roots did not have hyphae. At last, the identity of the

The seedlings with mushrooms growing nearby were all healthy.

mysterious soil factor was revealed. It had been the root fungi mushrooms all along.

Proof of the important role of root fungi led to many more studies. Scientists soon discovered that the root fungi do take sugars from plant roots, but they also help the plants get minerals from the soil. Today scientists think that most of the plants on Earth form partnerships with certain mushrooms, toadstools, and truffles. Many plants, like pine trees, cannot grow without their fungi partners.

The connections between root fungi and plants might have remained nature's secret. But its discovery changed the way that many people look at mushrooms and other fungi. Root fungi were once overlooked and often considered harmful parasites. But today these same organisms are recognized as important and valuable parts of nature.

People often consider certain parts of nature good and other parts as bad. But as ecologists learn more about the invisible connections in nature, this view is changing. Living things that seem bad, or of little value, are often surprisingly important.

THE MICE,
THE ANTS, AND
THE DESERT PLANTS

SCIENTISTS HAVE NOTICED that usually no two kinds of animals that live in the same area eat exactly the same kinds of foods. But in one desert area south of Tucson, Arizona, Diane Davidson and James Brown found seven species of ants and five species of mice all eating seeds of the same desert annual plants. This seemed particularly puzzling because seeds of these plants are often in short supply.

In the desert, scorching heat and lack of water make it difficult for any living things to survive. Annual plants survive only because they spend most of the year buried as seeds. These sprout and grow only after a heavy rain. Then the young plants have just a few weeks to grow roots and leaves, form flowers, and set seed. When the sands dry out again, the plants die and only the seeds survive. For an entire year the ants and mice must live on whatever seeds the plants have made during their short lives.

Considering this, Davidson and Brown suspected that desert ants and mice had to be in a sort of race, or competition, for the limited supply of seeds. They figured that if competition was happening, then the number of ants would affect the number of mice, and vice versa. To find out if their suspicions were correct, they set up eight experimental plots.

They removed all the mice from two small plots of desert. They built a fence around these plots to keep other mice from moving in. Then they set up two more plots and removed all the ants from these. In two other plots they removed both the mice and the ants. In their last two plots, their controls, they did not make any changes. Then the scientists waited to see what would happen to the mice and the ants in their plots.

One year later Davidson and Brown saw some obvious changes. There were twice as many ants in the plots where the mice had been removed. And in the plot where ants had been removed, the number of mice had increased. But there were no changes in ant or mice numbers in the control plots. These results proved that desert ants and mice do compete for food. When either kind of animal was re-

Ants and mice had a complicated relationship in their desert habitat.

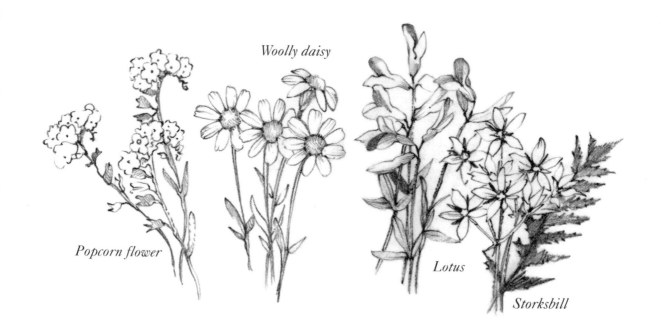

Woolly daisy

Popcorn flower

Lotus

Storksbill

moved, more seeds were left for the other species to eat. And whichever species got more food increased in number.

It seemed like an open-and-shut case, but Davidson and Brown knew that they might learn more if they continued the experiment for more than one year. So they kept the experimental plots in place and watched to see what would happen.

After a few years of watching events in the plots, the ecologists realized that something more than competition between ants and mice was happening. In the plots without mice, ant numbers did not remain high. Instead, ant numbers went down every year after the first. After four years few ants remained in the plots with no mice.

Not only that, the plant species inside these plots had changed. Pink-flowered storksbill and yellow-flowered lotus plants now covered the plots. But several other annual plants, like the tiny popcorn flower and woolly daisy, had become much less common. This was a result that Davidson and Brown had not expected. What had happened to the ants? And why had the desert plants changed?

The other plots yielded some clues. There were no changes in the numbers of ants, mice, or plants in the control plots. And in the plots with no ants the number of mice remained high, but the plants had not changed. There was a striking change in the plots with no ants or mice, though. These plots were overflowing with flowers of all kinds, though storksbill and lotus were most numerous. This showed that without ants and mice around to eat their seeds, more annual seeds had survived the long desert droughts to burst into bloom. This made Davidson and Brown realize that mice and ants not only affected each other, they also affected desert plants.

Considering the effects of the seed-eaters, the ecologists partly understood the changes in their plots with no mice. Mice prefer to eat large seeds. So it made sense that large-seeded storksbill and lotus had done well in plots with no mice. But why had popcorn flower, woolly daisy, and other annuals with small seeds become less common in the plots with no mice?

The scientists figured that in the plot with ants, the ants might have eaten most of the small seeds of these plants during the first year of the experiment when ant numbers were high. But ant numbers had gone down during the second and third years of the study. It seemed that popcorn flower, woolly daisy, and other small-seeded species should have become more common as ant numbers went down. Davidson and Brown were puzzled that the opposite had happened.

They discussed the problem with other desert scientists. A co-worker, R. S. Inouye, had a clue to the puzzle. He had discovered competition between different kinds of annual plants. He found that seedlings from large seeds grew their roots and leaves faster than seedlings from small seeds. This allowed the large-seeded seedlings to get more of the scarce rainwater and soil nutrients. And it allowed large-seeded plants to crowd out plants with small seeds. That was the clue Davidson and Brown needed to make sense out of the strange events in their experimental plots.

Removal of the mice had changed many things. Without mice, ants had more seeds to eat, so their numbers grew. The ants ate some large seeds, but not enough. So most of the seeds of large-seeded plants survived the drought. When the rains came, hundreds of the large-seed-ed storksbill and lotus sprouted. These seedlings crowded out the few popcorn flower, woolly daisy, and other small-seeded annuals that sprouted from seeds the ants had not eaten. Over the years the small-seeded annual plants were gradually crowded out. That left the ants without enough small seeds to eat. So the ants became scarce, too.

People tend to think animals only affect other kinds of animals by eating them. And we tend to think that preda-tors always reduce the numbers of their prey. But Davidson and Brown's experiments in the desert showed that nature's connections are not so simple.

Ants don't eat mice. And mice don't eat ants. Yet the number of mice affects the number of ants. Mice compete with ants for food and keep the numbers of ants down. Yet in the long run, more ants exist if mice are around. Similar-ly, small-seeded desert plants survive in part because of mice that eat their seeds. Davidson and Brown's experi-ments showed that when mice were not around to eat seeds, small-seeded annuals, like popcorn flower and wool-ly daisy, barely survived due to competition with large-seeded plants. Nature's connections are tangled indeed!

THE CASE
OF THE
RESTORED FOREST

WHEN PIONEERS FIRST SETTLED Wisconsin more than 150 years ago, the region was covered with forests of giant maple and oak trees. These forests were gradually cleared to make room for pastures, farmlands, houses, and cities. By the 1930s, little forestland remained in Wisconsin. The loss of forests from the state concerned scientists at the University of Wisconsin. They decided to try to reverse the process of forest loss by attempting to restore a natural forest to some pastureland owned by the university.

To restore the natural forest, the scientists planted hundreds of oak and maple trees along with many native shrubs in a pattern similar to that found in natural forests.

They also planted clusters of native wild flowers along several paths through the woods. The scientists hoped that their restored forest eventually would look just like a natural forest.

But fifty years later, when plant scientist Brock Woods walked through the restored forest, he knew something was wrong. As expected, the oak and maple trees had grown quite tall, and dappled sunlight filtered through their leaves just as in a natural forest. But the forest floor did not look natural. Clusters of bloodroot and ginger flowers grew along the trails where they had been planted fifty years earlier. But elsewhere in the forest these plants were nearly absent. That seemed peculiar to Woods because ginger and bloodroot flowers grew everywhere in Wisconsin's remaining natural forests. What had gone wrong in the restored forest? Woods wondered. Why had these flowering plants failed to spread away from the trails?

Woods thought carefully about the problem. Like most plants, ginger and bloodroot spread to new sites mainly by seeds. Some plant seeds, like those of dandelions, have tiny parachutes so they can float away to new places on the wind. Other plants, like burrs, produce seeds covered with tiny hooks. The hooks latch onto the fur of passing animals or the socks of unsuspecting people. That way they get a free ride to a new place. Some plants, like raspberry, produce berries. Their hard-coated seeds are inside the berry.

When an animal eats the berry, it digests only the sweet, fleshy part. The hard-coated seed passes unharmed through the animal's stomach. It ends up in the animal's droppings in a new place—with a bit of fertilizer.

When Woods examined the seeds of ginger and blood-root, he noticed that they didn't have parachutes to float on the wind, or stickers to latch on to fur, or fleshy berries to attract animals. Instead the seeds of these plants had a fatty coating, or lump, called an elaiosome (el-AY-o-som).

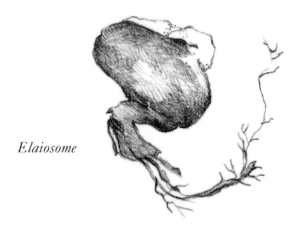

Elaiosome

This fatty material on a seed often attracts certain ants to carry the seed back to their nests. There the ants chew off the fatty lump and toss the seed into what amounts to an underground ant garbage dump. Two plant scientists, A. J. Beattie and D. C. Culver, found that fat-coated seeds of certain plants grew best if the seeds were first carried off by ants, chewed, then dumped in an ant garbage pit.

Woods decided he should find out more about the ants of the restored forest and their effects on the seeds of wild ginger and bloodroot.

Ants that eat fatty seed coatings are attracted to the seeds by the smell of the fat. Beattie and Culver showed that oil from tuna fish attracts the ants, too. So Woods set out some oily tuna fish as ant bait. In the restored forest, Woods watched the bait for several hours, but only a few ants came to investigate. Next Woods placed some tuna fish oil out in a patch of natural forest. The difference was spectacular. In just a short while hundreds of ants swarmed around the tuna fish. Through repeated tests Woods figured out that the natural forest had more than two hundred times the fat-eating ants than did the restored forest.

That led Woods to suspect that a shortage of ants might be the key to the mystery. But he was still puzzled. Even

without ants to scatter their seeds, some of the ginger and bloodroot seeds should have sprouted near the parent plants. Yet very few young plants grew in the restored woods—even right next to the parent clumps. Woods needed to do some more detective work to solve the mystery.

He set up an experiment to find out exactly what happened to ginger and bloodroot seeds. First he collected many seeds from both kinds of plants. Then he prepared two kinds of holders. The first holder was a flat mesh screen that made it easier to see and keep track of the seeds he placed out on the ground. He made a second type of holder, similar to a small cage, to keep mice and other seed-eating animals away from the seeds. Ants would still be able to get the seeds, but larger creatures would be kept away.

Once all the screens and cages were finished, Woods placed several of the flat screens and small cages out on the ground in a natural forest. Then he placed several seeds of ginger and bloodroot on each screen and inside each cage. After that, Woods sat down to watch. Hundreds of ants soon scurried out of the woods, onto the screens, and into the cages. They hoisted the seeds onto their backs and carried them off. Within an hour all the seeds were gone.

Woods repeated his experiment in the restored forest. He set out several flat screens and small cages. He placed several seeds of each plant species on the screens and in the cages. Then he sat down to observe. Hour after hour passed. No ants came by. No seeds were carried away. Finally the sun went down. Woods could no longer watch, so he went home to sleep.

When Woods returned the next morning, the seeds he had left on the flat screens were gone. Had the ants come during the night and finally carried the seeds away? Or had the seeds been eaten by mice? A few seed husks scattered around the screens hinted that mice were involved. The cages proved it. Inside the wire mesh, where mice could not reach, all the seeds remained.

Woods had solved the mystery. Ginger and bloodroot were not spreading in the restored forest due to an absence of ants. These particular plants need ants to scatter their seeds. Apparently they also need ants to hide their seeds from hungry mice. Woods thought he might be able to get the plants to spread by transplanting some ants to the restored forest. But so far his attempts to bring in the ants have failed. Now Woods is wondering why ants don't live in the restored forest. Is there something they need that is missing? That mystery remains to be solved.

It is easy to break the connections in nature by changing natural environments. But as the case of the restored forest shows, it is much easier to take nature apart than to put it back together.

THE PUZZLE OF THE VANISHING BUTTERFLIES

WITH WINGS OF BLUE spotted in red and black, the large blue butterfly was a living jewel of the English countryside. It lived in meadows where it sipped nectar from the purple flowers of thyme, a British wild flower. Once fairly common in southern England, the large blue became rare as English meadows were changed into farmlands and housing areas for people. The species survived in only thirty meadows by the early 1950s.

People concerned about the future of the large blue had set up nature reserves for it. In these reserves, meadows were protected from plows and houses. Butterfly collecting was strictly forbidden, and cows, sheep, and horses were removed as an added precaution. Naturalists were certain that the butterflies would survive as long as their meadow homes were protected. But between 1950 and 1960, large blues vanished from twenty-six of the thirty meadows, including most of the nature reserves.

No one could explain why the butterflies were disappearing. All the meadows had thyme plants for the butterflies to feed on. Despite increased efforts to save them, the butterflies soon disappeared from all but two meadows. In desperation, the people trying to save the butterfly called in Dr. Jeremy Thomas. They hoped Thomas, an expert in insect biology, could figure out why all efforts to save the beautiful insect had failed.

Thomas began his investigation of the mystery by reviewing what was already known about the butterfly's life cycle. Like other butterflies, adult large blues feed on flower nectar. They lay their eggs on thyme flowers, usually one egg per plant. The caterpillars that hatch from the eggs feed on the flowers of the thyme for about three weeks. Then something unusual occurs. In early evening the caterpillars drop to the ground and begin giving off a sweet chemical. This chemical attracts certain red ants. When an ant finds a caterpillar, it begins to feed on the chemical. After several hours of feeding, the ant picks up the caterpillar and carries it down into the ant's nest.

Once inside an ant nest, the caterpillar of the large blue eats ant larvae. No one knows why the ants put up with this. But for some reason they do. So the caterpillar continues to grow. Still inside the ant nest, the caterpillar hibernates through winter. In spring it awakens and eats more ant larvae.

Then, like all butterfly larvae, the large blue caterpillar grows a tough skin, called a chrysalis. (A chrysalis is like a cocoon.) Inside the chrysalis the caterpillar's body changes shape. It turns from a wormlike caterpillar into the beautiful winged form of an adult. Only then does the insect leave the ant nest to feed on flower nectar. After a while the adult butterflies mate, the females lay eggs, and the cycle begins again.

The unusual life of the large blue butterfly included many mysteries. But Thomas had little time and few butterflies. He had to concentrate on the mystery of the butterflies' disappearance. Thomas figured that the butterflies would disappear if any link in their life cycle was broken. So he decided to trace the butterflies through their life cycle and look for any breaks in the chain of events.

He began by looking at the adult butterflies. Did they have enough food? Were there enough places to lay eggs? Thomas looked at the two meadows where large blues still lived. The purple flowers of wild thyme dotted both meadows. Next Thomas looked at the meadows where large

Large blue caterpillar on wild thyme

blues no longer lived. Wild thyme dotted most of them, too. It was missing from a few meadows where shrubs and scrub trees had moved in. But overall Thomas had to conclude that lack of food and egg-laying sites were not problems.

Were the eggs hatching out? Yes. Thomas found that while some eggs were lost to predators and parasites, most survived to hatch. The caterpillars appeared normal, and they seemed to have plenty to eat. Many were killed by predators, but many others survived.

Thomas discovered the first clue to the mystery when he looked at the connection between large blues and ants. After hours and hours of watching and studying the ants and the caterpillars, Thomas noticed something surprising.

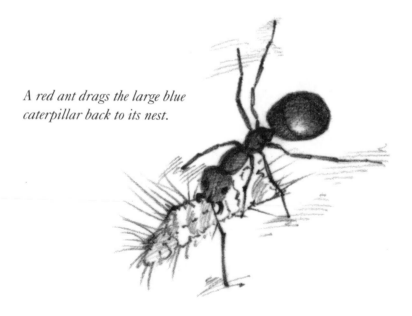

A red ant drags the large blue caterpillar back to its nest.

Two different kinds of red ants were hauling large blue caterpillars off to their underground nests. But for some reason the caterpillars survived in the nests of only one of the ant species.

Thomas immediately began looking more carefully at the ants in various meadows. By this time large blues remained in just one meadow. In this meadow Thomas found many of the ants needed by the large blue. When he looked at the meadows where large blues no longer lived, he found mostly the other species of ant. The right ants were uncommon or absent. This evidence showed that large blue butterflies could only live in meadows with lots of the right ants. Thomas needed to find out what events might cause a change in the kinds of ants in a meadow.

After studying the two kinds of ants and their habitats, he discovered that the ants that help large blue caterpillars only lived in meadows with short grasses. When tall grasses, shrubs, or trees moved into the meadow, the ants needed by large blue butterflies disappeared. And the ants that didn't help the butterflies moved in. After looking more closely at several meadows, Thomas realized that tall grasses and shrubs quickly moved into any meadows without grazing animals.

As Thomas considered this information he looked back over the history of the large blue's disappearance. The 1950s stood out as the time of the species' worst decline. In those ten years alone the butterflies had disappeared from twenty-six different meadows in the country. Why might the ant populations have suddenly changed in all those meadows in those years?

Thomas didn't have to think very hard to solve the mystery. Rabbits had nearly disappeared from England in the 1950s. A rabbit disease called myxomatosis had been brought in from Europe. It spread like wildfire through the rabbits of the English countryside. And nearly all of them had died. Thomas quickly recognized the missing piece of the butterfly puzzle.

He put the pieces together this way. The disease wiped out all the rabbits. Without hungry rabbits eating the grasses, tall grasses and shrubs began to grow in all the meadows where cows and sheep were absent. That included the nature reserves, where people had kept cattle and sheep out in hopes of protecting the large blue. When the tall grasses and shrubs moved in, the right ants were forced out. Even though the adult butterflies had plenty of thyme plants for food and laying eggs, the caterpillars could not survive. They needed the missing ants. Without the right ants to care for them, the caterpillars died. Thus the cycle ended, and the species disappeared.

Once Thomas figured out the complicated connections, it seemed that it might be easy to save the one remaining large blue colony by bringing in rabbits or other grazing animals. He hoped it would bring back the ants, and the butterflies. Sadly, though, it was already too late. In the four years of Thomas's investigation, most of the remaining large blues had disappeared. In the next few years, poor weather, predators, and overcrowding of the remaining ant nests killed off the last few large blues.

So the large blue butterfly is gone from Great Britain. It disappeared due to changes in land use by people and because of a rabbit disease. That is how the tangled connections of nature work sometimes.

Earth has millions of secret connections like those among large blue butterflies, ants, plants, and rabbits. Ecologists may never know them all. But unless we try to understand these secret connections, the butterflies and other beautiful creatures that share our planet will continue to disappear.

THE DISAPPEARING PEREGRINES

PERCHED ON A CLIFF-TOP BRANCH, a peregrine falcon peers out from a black tear-drop mask. It surveys the air, the rivers, and forests below. Catching sight of a robin, the falcon lifts off and soars upward to the clouds. Abruptly changing course, it dives. With deadly aim it rockets to a speed of 180 miles per hour. A split second later the peregrine carries its lifeless prey back to a perch. Robin feathers flutter downwind as the peregrine dines.

Bird watchers, falconers, and scientists around the world have watched many such scenes. The peregrine falcon was once one of the most common and widespread birds of prey in the world. But something went wrong during the 1950s. Nesting pairs began to lay fewer eggs. Fewer young hatched. And each year a few more nest sites were abandoned. No one understood why it was happening, but the species was disappearing from many parts of the world. Concerned scientists held a meeting in 1964 to discuss the mystery.

It seemed that every scientist at the meeting suspected a different cause. Some suspected predators like raccoons had destroyed nests. Others blamed rock climbers who disturbed nesting birds. Some scientists pointed to the large number of falcons shot by people. Others blamed a change in climate. Each of these culprits did seem to be involved in the disappearance of falcons from certain places. But something seemed odd about the case. Why would unrelated events cause declines in peregrines in so many parts of the world all at once?

A British scientist at the meeting, Derek Ratcliffe, suggested that it was more likely a single culprit was harming peregrines everywhere. He thought he knew the identity of the culprit. The only problem was that he didn't have proof. All he had was a hunch and some shaky evidence.

Ratcliffe had collected records of peregrine nests from observers throughout Great Britain while investigating an increase in the number of complaints about the predators from pigeon fanciers. Based on the pigeon fanciers' reports, Ratcliffe had expected to find that peregrine numbers were growing. What he found instead was that in recent years peregrine falcons throughout all of Great Britain had failed to raise young. Now the peregrines were disappearing. Since the decline in peregrines had begun at the same time throughout Britain, Ratcliffe suspected that a widespread environmental change had caused the peregrines' disappearance.

In his efforts to identify possible suspects, Ratcliffe noticed that widespread use of certain chemicals, called pesticides, had begun about the same time as the peregrine nesting failures. Farmers spread these pesticides to kill insects that harm their crops. Ratcliffe had a hunch that some pesticides killed peregrines as well as insects.

As Ratcliffe studied the records of nest failures, he discovered some evidence that tied pesticides to the crime scene. Peregrine nest failures began earlier and were more frequent in southern Britain than in northern Britain. That fit. Pesticides were widely used in the rich farmlands of southern Britain. In contrast, pesticides were rarely used in northern Britain, where poor soils limited farming. This evidence was just circumstantial, but it made Ratcliffe more suspicious.

To prove his case Ratcliffe needed better evidence. Laboratory studies showed that the small amounts of pesticides in the air, water, and soil of Britain were far too low to kill peregrines. However, scientists in another part of the world had made a surprising discovery.

California scientists had measured concentrations of the pesticide DDT in wildlife after it was sprayed on a lake. Almost no trace of the pesticide occurred in the water and plant life of the lake. And only minute traces appeared in lake wildlife. But plant life around the lake contained a much higher concentration of the pesticide than the water. Animals that ate plants contained more of this pesticide than found in plants. And animals that ate other animals contained far more of this pesticide than plant-eating animals.

This concentration of a pesticide through a food chain hinted of danger to peregrines. Peregrines eat other birds, which eat insects, which eat plants. They are at the top of the food chain. Ratcliffe suspected that peregrines might have high levels of certain pesticides in their tissues despite the extremely low levels of these chemicals in the environment.

To find out, he collected eggs from failed peregrine nests and sent them to chemical laboratories for analysis. He sent dead peregrines to labs for analysis. He also sent in bodies of songbirds, shorebirds, and seabirds—all prey of the peregrine.

The results of these tests were confusing. Minute traces of several pesticides, including DDT, were found in the peregrines' prey. Concentrations in peregrine eggs and tissues were much higher than in their prey. And they were

far higher than in the air, water, and soil. This showed that these pesticides were indeed reaching peregrines through the food chain.

But even so, pesticide concentrations in the peregrines and their eggs were extremely tiny. Since laboratory tests showed tiny doses did not kill birds, it seemed that Ratcliffe's analyses had proved his own hunch wrong.

Still Ratcliffe remained suspicious of pesticides. He presented his incomplete case to the other scientists at the 1964 meeting. First he presented the circumstantial evidence tying pesticides to the time and place of the peregrine decline. Next he pointed out that the peregrine decline in Britain had begun with nesting failures. After 1951, breakage of eggs, desertion of eggs, and failure of eggs to hatch were the most frequent causes of nest failure. Ratcliffe pointed out that breakage of eggs was most often blamed on an adult peregrine eating the egg. In conclusion he stated, "I believe that in some direct or indirect way, which I do not pretend to understand, this abnormal . . . [egg-eating] behavior is occasioned by sublethal [not deadly] doses of pesticides. . . ."

To many scientists at the meeting, Ratcliffe's ideas seemed too far-fetched. Many environmental changes had occurred at the same time as the peregrine falcon nesting failures. Extremely tiny amounts of pesticides had been proven safe in laboratory tests. And other explanations of the peregrine decline were much easier for most people to believe.

Despite these arguments, Ratcliffe's ideas caused several scientists to add pesticides to their own suspect lists. They began testing for pesticides in falcons in other parts of the world. Within a year test results were back. Tiny traces of certain pesticides existed in peregrines everywhere. Most startling was the discovery of DDT and related pesticides in birds from remote Alaska and Canada. This showed that these pesticides had spread thousands of miles from farmers' fields to the far corners of the earth. But it was still not proof that pesticides were guilty.

Not surprisingly, the detective who first sniffed out the suspect also uncovered the case-breaking clue. One day, while holding a broken egg from a failed nest, Ratcliffe noticed that the shell seemed unusually fragile. He quickly weighed and measured eggs from several falcon nests that

had recently failed. All seemed light and fragile. Next he visited museums and egg-collectors to examine eggs they had collected in previous years.

When he compared all these measurements, he discovered that all the eggs collected after 1947 had thinner shells than eggs collected in previous years. Joseph Hickey, an American scientist, repeated Ratcliffe's study in the United States. He found the same striking change in North American falcon eggs. What had happened in 1947 to cause this worldwide change in eggshell thickness? Ratcliffe and Hickey thought they knew. In 1947 widespread use of DDT and similar pesticides had begun.

If it could be shown that these pesticides caused birds to lay thin-shelled eggs, the case would be solved. Scientists quickly began the needed experiments. United States Department of Agriculture scientists K. L. Davison and J. L. Sell fed tiny doses of DDT and similar pesticides to mallard ducks. The extremely low doses did not kill the mallards or make them sick. But unbelievably tiny doses did cause the ducks to lay thin-shelled eggs. Much higher levels of these pesticides had been found in peregrines. So the case was clinched.

Ratcliffe's hunch about pesticides was proved correct, though his first guess about the effects of the pesticides had been wrong. Peregrines ate their eggs only because the thin-shelled eggs broke during nesting. It took scientists over twenty years to catch the killers, but DDT and similar pesticides were finally proved guilty. In the meantime, eggshell thinning led to the near extinction of peregrines and severe declines in populations of bald eagles, osprey, brown pelicans, and other predatory birds. The work of Ratcliffe and other scientists led to laws banning the use of DDT and similar pesticides in the United States and Europe. These laws, combined with an intensive restoration effort, are slowly bringing back all the affected bird species.

As the peregrine falcon returns, ecologists hope that people will not forget the mystery of its disappearance. The peregrine's plight warned that extremely tiny amounts of certain man-made chemicals have deadly, hidden effects. It showed that some chemicals become concentrated by the invisible food chain connections that tie all living things together. And it proved that no region of the earth is unaffected. For as Roger Tory Peterson, the famous bird scientist, observed, "As long as winds blow, or fishes swim, or birds travel, [some man-made] chemicals will move . . . to the ends of the earth."

THE MYSTERY OF THE MISSING SONGS

ONLY OBSERVANT BIRD WATCHERS notice it, but the sound of spring has changed in the northeastern United States. Forests that once overflowed with songbird music now sound different. Jays still call, and wrens and robins still sing, but the trills of warblers, chirps of flycatchers, whistles of tanagers, and the fluted songs of thrushes are gone. Some of the most colorful North American songbirds have disappeared from most of our eastern forests.

When ecologists first began investigating the birds' mysterious disappearance, they suspected that loss of forest habitat was the problem. Forest birds need forests to live, and great changes have occurred in northeastern forests. Where vast expanses of trees once stood, people have cleared the land to make room for highways, houses, shopping centers, airports, and farms. The remaining forest patches are like islands surrounded by a sea of human-altered landscapes.

Several scientists figured that the remaining forest islands were too small to provide feeding and nesting sites for the missing songbirds. In one study, Bruce Whitcomb and his co-workers counted the birds in several protected forests in Maryland. They found that the missing songbird species were completely absent from small forest patches, yet they still occurred in large forest reserves.

The absence of the birds from small forest patches mystified investigating scientists. The missing songbirds are all small birds. Even in a large forest each nesting pair only uses a few acres of forest. It seems that several pairs of birds might easily nest in a small twenty-to-fifty-acre patch of forest. So why were they missing from these small forest islands? Different scientists had various ideas.

David Wilcove suspected predators were somehow involved. He noticed that most of the remaining bird species nested in holes in trees, or built covered nests. In contrast, nearly all of the missing songbirds built open, cuplike nests of sticks or grass. Such open nests are easy for predators to rob. Wilcove also noticed that jays, raccoons, skunks, and other potential nest predators were common in areas where islands of forest were mixed with open fields, lawns, and farmland. He guessed that bird nests in small forest islands might be easier for predators to find than nests hidden in a large forest.

To test his idea, Wilcove made several artificial bird nests out of woven grass and put three quail eggs in each nest. He placed these egg-filled nests in spots where the missing songbirds might nest.

He put many of the nests out in small forest patches surrounded by open areas and buildings. He placed the rest of the artificial nests out in large forest expanses, including the forest of Great Smoky Mountains National Park. Wilcove checked the nests a few days after placing them out. Nearly all the nests in the large forest tract still contained eggs. But in the small forest patches, almost every single artificial nest placed out was empty.

To figure out what predators were stealing the eggs, Wilcove had spread soot, modeling clay, and other materials around some artificial nests with eggs. The nest predators revealed themselves by leaving tracks. Jays, raccoons, opossums, skunks, domestic cats and dogs were all culprits. Wilcove's clever experiment showed that predators were certainly involved in the case of the missing songbirds.

A cowbird throws an egg out of a songbird's nest to make room for its own.

Meanwhile, though, Harold Mayfield and other researchers had focused their investigation on another suspect—the brown-headed cowbird. Cowbirds live in open areas but move into forests during the nesting season. Instead of building its own nest in the forest, a female cowbird looks for the nest of another songbird. Warblers, thrushes, flycatchers, and tanagers are all at risk. When one of these species has built a nest and laid eggs, the cowbird keeps a close watch. When the female leaves her nest to feed, the cowbird sneaks in. She lays her own egg in the nest. Sometimes the cowbird throws out one or more of the other eggs to make room for her own egg.

When the nesting bird returns, she often does not notice the new egg. So she sits on the cowbird egg along with her own eggs. When the cowbird chick hatches, the nesting bird mistakenly feeds it. Usually the cowbird chick is bigger than the other chicks in the nest. It may kill the other chicks, crowd them out, or hog all of the food the parent birds bring back. Often the cowbird chick is the only chick in the nest that survives.

Mayfield suspected that cowbirds might be involved in the disappearance of the songbirds because their numbers have skyrocketed in recent years. Cowbirds live in open areas. And they eat grain. The grain farms that have replaced the forest in many parts of the eastern United States make perfect living sites for cowbirds.

Other scientists uncovered evidence that clearly links an increase in cowbirds to the decrease in certain songbird populations. Bird scientists Margaret Brittingham and Stanley Temple discovered cowbird eggs in sixty-five out of one hundred nests of the missing songbirds. They also found that nests near a forest edge were more likely to contain cowbird eggs than nests placed deep inside a large forest. In Illinois, researcher Scott Robinson found cowbird eggs in twenty-nine of thirty wood thrush nests. In Maryland, scientist Russell Greenberg reported cowbird eggs in every single worm-eating warbler nest that he examined over a two-year period. These and other findings suggest that many songbirds are raising cowbird chicks instead of their own young. Cowbirds are clearly involved in the case of the disappearing songbirds, too.

However, just as the involvement of predators and cowbirds became clear, another suspect was brought forward. George Hall and other bird watchers in West Virginia reported that the number of songbird species had gone down even in a large expanse of forest that they studied. In this case predators and cowbirds did not seem to be involved. Hall and his co-workers noted that all the missing songbird species were long-distance migrants. These birds nest in the United States, then fly thousands of miles south to winter in Mexico and Central or South America. Hall's group suggested that the birds might be disappearing due to loss of their winter homes.

Nearly one-third of the tropical forests on their wintering grounds have been cut down by people in just the last forty years. And forest clearing continues at an alarming rate. Without tropical forest to live in during winter, many North American songbirds cannot survive throughout the year.

Today most bird scientists agree that predators, cowbirds, and loss of northern and tropical forests are all involved in the case of the disappearing songbirds. It looks as if there is no single culprit to blame. On second glance, however, one culprit comes to mind. Each of the changes that have led to problems for the songbirds can be traced to environmental changes made by people. When people changed the forest expanses of the east into a patchwork of forest islands, predation on songbird nests by jays, skunks, raccoons, and domestic cats increased. By creating farmland and raising grain crops, people also improved living conditions for cowbirds. This caused the explosion in their numbers. People are also the agents clearing the tropical forests that many songbirds need to survive in winter.

When you throw a stone into a pond, small waves ripple outward. Every change we make in nature causes ripples, too. It remains to be seen whether we can save the disappearing songbirds of eastern North America. But there is hope, now that scientists understand some of the connections between human-caused habitat changes and the missing songs in the spring chorus.

Ovenbird

Kentucky warbler

Scarlet tanager

Yellow-throated vireo

Northern parula
warbler

Cerulean warbler

Northern oriole

Black-and-white warbler

Least
flycatcher

Hooded warbler

Veery

THE CASE OF THE TWIN ISLANDS

AMCHITKA AND SHEMYA ISLANDS lie close together in the Aleutian Island chain in the Gulf of Alaska. Both islands are made of the same kinds of rocks, and the same kind of rocky ocean floor occurs around each island. They are both surrounded by clear, unpolluted waters of the same temperature and saltiness. The marine environments of the two islands are nearly identical. However, the two islands are home to very different groups of marine plants and animals. Marine scientists James Estes, Norman Smith, and John Palmisano wondered how the islands could be so alike, and yet so different.

These scientists could explain just one difference in the life around the two islands. Amchitka Island is home to several thousand sea otters, while none live around Shemya. This difference is due to history. Sea otters are large fur-bearing marine mammals. Their fur is one of the softest and warmest furs in the world, so sea otters were once hunted by people. In the late 1800s, fur traders from Russia, Asia, and North America searched for otters in every bay and inlet of western North America. They killed all the otters they found in order to get their furs. They nearly killed off all the sea otters on Earth.

Fortunately, however, a few sea otters escaped the hunters. These otters survived in hidden coves in Alaska and in Monterey Bay, California. After decades of protection from fur traders, sea otters had slowly returned to their former abundance in a few areas, including the waters around Amchitka Island. But they had not returned yet to Shemya Island.

Estes, Smith, and Palmisano suspected that sea otters might be the cause of all the other differences in marine life around Amchitka and Shemya Islands. To find out if their hunch was right, these scientists visited both islands and dived around them several times. They counted the numbers, sizes, and kinds of marine plants and animals around each island.

Amchitka Island, home to thousands of sea otters, was

also home to hundreds of seals. There, bald eagles swooped low over the sea to catch fish in their talons. Underwater the scientists found a forest of giant kelp, a kind of marine plant. Huge brown fronds of the kelp rose up from the ocean bottom toward the sunlit surface. Many shrimplike animals and lots of fish lived amidst the waving kelp fronds. But few animals lived on the ocean bottom.

In contrast, Shemya Island, which had no sea otters, also had few seals and no bald eagles. Underwater the biologists found almost no kelp, few shrimplike animals, and few fish. But here, the ocean bottom was swarming with sea urchins, chitons, limpets, blue mussels, and barnacles.

The scientists couldn't figure out what was going on without knowing more about the connections among the ocean creatures. So they read many reports by other scientists. Information about the food of sea otters gave the ecologists their first clue.

Sea otters dive underwater to catch their food, which includes many kinds of marine animals. Sea urchins are one of their favorite foods. Because they are large animals, sea otters need a lot of food. A single adult sea otter must eat nine to thirteen pounds of marine animals every day. Estes's team quickly realized that a population of thousands of sea otters would soon eat all the large marine animals within their reach. That explained why few sea urchins were found near Amchitka Island. Any urchins

A kelp forest and many sea otters surround Amchitka Island.

within easy reach of the diving sea otters had been eaten there. But around Shemya Island there were no sea otters to eat them, so the sea urchins thrived.

What difference did it make that sea otters had eaten most of the sea urchins around Amchitka? Since sea urchins graze on kelp and algae, Estes's team suspected that sea urchins might affect the kelp. Studies by other scientists proved that their suspicions were correct.

Sea urchins not only eat kelp, they also gnaw through the bases of kelp fronds. This breaks the kelp's anchor hold on the ocean bottom, and the urchin-gnawed kelp soon washes ashore to die. When lots of sea urchins are around, they eat through all the bases of the giant kelp. So kelp cannot grow on a site patrolled by hordes of sea urchins. That explained the absence of kelp on Shemya, where the ocean bottom was carpeted with giant sea urchins. It also explained why kelp had formed an underwater forest on Amchitka, where sea otters had eaten all the large urchins.

The scientists soon tied other differences in the animal life of the two islands to the presence and absence of the kelp forest. Shrimplike amphipods and isopods live in calm waters and feast on dead kelp. The kelp forest of Amchitka provided a perfect habitat for these animals. In contrast, bottom-dwelling animals were smothered by the sand and silt that settled in waters calmed by Amchitka's kelp forest.

Many kinds of fish prey on shrimplike animals, but few

Sea urchins thrive around Shemya Island.

fish can eat bottom-dwelling animals like sea urchins, chitons, barnacles, or mussels. Consequently fish were more numerous in the kelp forest of Amchitka than in the waters around Shemya. Harbor seals and bald eagles eat fish. So they were more numerous around Amchitka, too.

Estes's team concluded that when the sea otters around Amchitka Island had eaten all the big sea urchins, the kelp forest was allowed to grow. The kelp forest in turn provided habitat and food for shrimplike animals, which then became food for fish. Fish, in turn, provided food for seals and eagles. So all the amazing differences in the marine life around Amchitka and Shemya Islands could be traced to the presence or absence of a single animal species—the sea otter.

When stone layers build an archway, they place a single, wedge-shaped stone at the top of the arch. This single stone keeps the other rocks in place and holds the arch together. If the keystone is removed, the archway falls apart. Ecologists had long suspected that certain species were keystones of living communities. The investigations of Estes's team showed that sea otters are a keystone in the North Pacific. Through a tangle of connections, sea otters affect many other parts of the world. Populations of kelp, invertebrate animals, fish, seals, and eagles are tied indirectly, but indivisibly, to the welfare of sea otters.

The fur traders of the 1800s had no idea that their relentless harvest of sea otters would cause dramatic changes in the marine environment. And in the 1960s, no one expected striking changes in the marine environment as sea otters returned to their former homes. But the removal, and addition, of this single animal species caused many dramatic changes.

Today ecologists recognize that all living things are tied together by invisible connections. And some species, like the sea otter, are keystones. As thousands of species of plants and animals become endangered or extinct due to the activities of humans, ecologists worry. Which of the rapidly disappearing species are keystones? And what unexpected changes will occur when the keystones are removed from nature's living arches?

A CLOSING NOTE

THE STORIES DESCRIBED in this book are about just a few of the connections in nature. Ecologists have discovered thousands upon thousands. Yet they are still investigating mysteries. They are still conducting experiments. And they are still discovering new connections.

Because of these connections, we cannot change one part of nature without affecting other parts. All of nature is tied together. Some scientists think that nature—our entire planet—is like a single living thing. Aldo Leopold called it the land organism.

The land organism is made up of all living and nonliving things and the connections between them. Human beings are part of it. We ourselves are tied by invisible threads to all the living and nonliving things on Earth. That makes it difficult for us to see the land organism. But it is there.

And now that you know about it, you'll begin to see it all around you. You may find it in tracks in the sand, or see it in the flight of a butterfly. You may spot it in a tide pool, or in a flock of passing birds. You may glimpse it in the scurry of an ant, or in the glow of a sunset. You might even see it in your mirror.

FOR FURTHER READING

Ecologists report investigations and discoveries in professional journals available in most university libraries. This list of references includes some of the original reports of scientists who investigated the mysteries described in this book.

The Mystery of Saint Matthew Island
Klein, D. R. 1959. "Saint Matthew Island Reindeer-Range Study." U.S. Fish and Wildlife Service. *Special Scientific Report—Wildlife* No. 43.
Klein, D. R. 1968. "The Introduction, Increase, and Crash of Reindeer on St. Matthew Island." *Journal of Wildlife Management* 32:350-367.
Klein, D. R. 1970. "An Alaskan Population Explosion." *Explorers Journal* 48:162-172.

The Secret of the Beautiful Butterflies
Brower, L. P. 1969. "Ecological Chemistry." *Scientific American* 220:22-29.
Brower, L. P., and J. Van Zandt Brower. 1964. "Birds, Butterflies, and Plant Poisons: A Study in Ecological Chemistry." *Zoologica* 49:137-159.

The Mystery of the Disappearing Hares
Bryant, J. P. 1981. "Hare Trigger." *Natural History* 90 (2):46-52.
Bryant, J. P. 1981. "Phytochemical Deterrence of Snowshoe Hare Browsing by Adventitious Shoots of Four Alaskan Trees." *Science* 213:889-890.

The Case of the Orange Feathers
Brush, A. H. 1990. "A Possible Source for the Rhodoxanthin in Some Cedar Waxwing Tails." *Journal of Field Ornithology* 61:355.
Hudon, J., and A. H. Brush. 1989. "Probable Dietary Basis of a Color Variant of the Cedar Waxwing." *Journal of Field Ornithology* 60:361-368.

The Puzzle in the Postcard Scene
Cantor, L. F., and T. G. Whitham. 1989. "Importance of Belowground *(sic)* Herbivory: Pocket Gophers May Limit Aspen to Rock Outcrop Refugia." *Ecology* 70:962-970.

The Riddle of the Green Tree Islands

Laine, K. J., and P. Niemelä. 1980. "The Influence of Ants on the Survival of Mountain Birches During an *Oporinia Autumnata* (Lep., Geometridae) Outbreak." *Oecologia* 47:39-42.

Niemelä, P., and K. J. Laine. 1986. "Green Islands—Predation Not Nutrition." *Oecologia* 68:476-478.

The Case of the Mummified Pigs

Payne, J. A. 1965. "A Summer Carrion Study of the Baby Pig *Sus Scrofa* Linnaeus." *Ecology* 46:592-602.

The Trees That Would Not Grow

Hacskaylo, E. 1967. "Mycorrhizae: Indispensable Invasions by Fungi." *Agricultural Science Review* 5:13-20.

Kessell, S. L. 1927. "Soil Organisms. The Dependence of Certain Pine Species on a Biological Soil Factor." *Empire Forestry Journal* 6:70-74.

Vozzo, J. A., and E. Hacskaylo. 1971. "Inoculation of *Pinus Caribaea* with Ecto-mycorrhizal Fungi in Puerto Rico." *Forest Science* 17:239-245.

The Mice, the Ants, and the Desert Plants

Brown, J. H., and D. W. Davidson. 1977. "Competition Between Seed-Eating Rodents and Ants in Desert Ecosystems." *Science* 196:880-882.

Davidson, D. W., R. S. Inouye, and J. H. Brown. 1984. "Granivory in a Desert Ecosystem: Experimental Evidence for Indirect Facilitation of Ants by Rodents." *Ecology* 65:1780-1786.

The Case of the Restored Forest

Culver, D. C., and A. J. Beattie. 1978. "Myrmecochory in Viola: Dynamics of Seed-Ant Interactions in Some West Virginia Species." *Journal of Ecology* 66:53-72.

Woods, B. 1984. "Ants Disperse Seed of Herb Species in a Restored Maple Forest (Wisconsin)." *Restoration and Management Notes* 2:29-30.

The Puzzle of the Vanishing Butterflies

Ratcliffe, D. A. 1979. "The End of the Large Blue." *New Scientist* 8:457-458.

Thomas, J. A. 1976. "The Ecology of the Large Blue Butterfly." *Annual Report of the Institute of Terrestrial Ecology*, pp. 25-27.

Thomas, J. A. 1979. "The Extinction of the Large Blue and the Conservation of the Black Hairstreak Butterflies (A Contrast of Failure and Success)." *Annual Report of the Institute of Terrestrial Ecology*, pp. 19-23.

Thomas, J. A. 1980. "Why Did the Large Blue Become Extinct in Britain?" *Oryx* 15:243-247.

The Disappearing Peregrines

Buckley, J. 1986. "Environmental Effects of DDT." Pages 358-374 in *Ecological Knowledge and Environmental Problem Solving: Concepts and Case Studies*, edited by National Research Council (U.S.), Commission on Life Sciences, Committee on Applications of Ecological Theory to Environmental Problems. Washington, D.C.: National Academy Press.

Davison, K. L., and J. L. Sell. 1974. "DDT Thins Shells of Eggs from Mallard Ducks Maintained on *Ad Libitum* or Controlled Feeding Regimens." *Archives of Environmental Contamination and Toxicology* 2:222-232.

Heath, R. G., J. W. Spann, J. K. Kreitzer. 1969. "Marked DDE Impairment of Mallard Reproduction in Controlled Studies." *Nature* 224:47-48.

Ratcliffe, D. A. 1963. "The Status of the Peregrine in Great Britain." *Bird Study* 10:56-90.

Ratcliffe, D. A. 1967. "Decrease in Eggshell Weight in Certain Birds of Prey." *Nature* 215:208-210.

Ratcliffe, D. A. 1969. "Population Trends of the Peregrine Falcon in Great Britain." Pages 239-269 in "Peregrine Falcon Populations," edited by J. J. Hickey. University of Wisconsin Press. Madison.

Ratcliffe, D. A. 1980. *The Peregrine Falcon*. Vermillion, South Dakota: Bueto Books.

The Mystery of the Missing Songs

Brittingham, M. C., and S. A. Temple. 1983. "Have Cowbirds Caused Forest Songbirds to Decline?" *Bioscience* 33:31-35.

Mayfield, H. 1977. "Brown-Headed Cowbird: Agent of Extermination?" *American Birds* 31:107-114.

Robbins, C. S. 1979. "Effects of Forest Fragmentation on Bird Populations." Pages 198-213 in "Management of North Central and Northeastern Forests for Nongame Birds," edited by R. M. DeGraaf and K. E. Evans. *U.S.D.A. Forest Service General Technical Report* NC 51.

Terborgh, J. 1989. *Where Have All the Birds Gone?* New Jersey: Princeton University Press. 207 pp.

Whitcomb, R. F. 1977. "Island Biogeography and 'Habitat Islands' of Eastern Forest." *American Birds* 31:3-5.

Whitcomb, R. F., C. S. Robbins, J. F. Lynch, B. L. Whitcomb, K. Klimkiewicz, and D. Bystrak. 1981. "Effects of Forest Fragmentation on Avifauna of the Eastern Deciduous Forest." Pages 125-205 in *Forest Island Dynamics in Man-Dominated Landscapes*, edited by R. L. Burgess and D. M. Sharpe. New York: Springer-Verlag.

Wilcove, D. S. 1985. "Nest Predation in Forest Tracts and the Decline of Migratory Songbirds." *Ecology* 66:1211-1214.

The Case of the Twin Islands

Estes, J. A., and J. F. Palmisano. 1974. "Sea Otters: Their Role in Structuring Nearshore Communities." *Science* 185:1058-1060.

Estes, J. A., N. S. Smith, and J. F. Palmisano. 1978. "Sea Otter Predation and Community Organization in Western Aleutian Islands, Alaska." *Ecology* 59:822-833.

Palmisano, J. F. 1983. "Sea Otter Predation: Its Role in Structuring Rocky Intertidal Communities in the Aleutian Islands, AK, U.S.A." *Acta Zoologica Fennica* 174:209-211.

More About Ecology

British Museum (Natural History). 1982. *Introducing Ecology: Nature at Work.* London: Cambridge University Press.

Facklam, Margery. 1989. *Partners for Life: The Mysteries of Animal Symbioses.* Boston: Sierra Club Books/Little, Brown.

Leopold, Aldo. 1970. *A Sand County Almanac with Essays on Conservation from Round River.* New York: Sierra Club/Ballantine.

Pollack, Steve. 1993. *Eyewitness Science: Ecology.* New York: Dorling-Kindersley.

Pringle, Laurence. 1987. *Restoring Our Earth.* Hillside, New Jersey: Enslow Publishers, Inc.

Pringle, Laurence. 1991. *Living Treasure: Saving Earth's Threatened Biodiversity.* New York: Morrow Junior Books.

Savan, Beth. 1991. *Earthwatch: Earthcycles and Ecosystems.* Reading, Massachusetts: Addison-Wesley Publishing Co.

INDEX